D1397829

21st Century Skills **INNOVATION** *Library*

Space Travel

by James M. Flammang

Published in the United States of America by Cherry Lake Publishing
Ann Arbor, Michigan
www.cherrylakepublishing.com

Content Adviser: Amy C. Newman, Director, Forney Museum of Transportation

Design: The Design Lab

Photo Credits: Cover and page 3, ©JUPITER IMAGES/Comstock Images/Alamy; pages 4, 7, 8, 11, 12, 19, 20, 22, 25, 27, and 28, Photo courtesy of NASA; page 15, ©AP Photo/John Raoux; page 16, ©iStockphoto.com/pastorscott; page 17, ©imac/Alamy; page 23, ©Michael Doolittle/Alamy; page 26, ©Photo Researchers/Alamy

Library of Congress Cataloging-in-Publication Data
Flammang, James M.
  Space travel / by James M. Flammang.
     p. cm.–(Innovation in transportation)
  Includes index.
  ISBN-13: 978-1-60279-232-6
  ISBN-10: 1-60279-232-1
  1. Astronautics–Technological innovations. 2. Outer space–Exploration. 3. Interplanetary voyages.
I. Title. II. Series.
  TL793.F55 2009
  629.45–dc22   2008003214

Cherry Lake Publishing would like to acknowledge the work of
The Partnership for 21st Century Skills.
Please visit www.21stcenturyskills.org for more information.

CONTENTS

Atlantis

USI

CHAPTER ONE

Space Travel

On July 20, 1969, Neil Armstrong became the first human to walk on the moon.

"Four. Three. Two. One. Liftoff!"

Nearly everyone with a television set knew what those words meant in 1969. The series of numbers was a countdown for the launch of an American spaceship that year. At least 100 million people were watching TV when the United States first sent **astronauts** into space to try to land on the Moon. Millions more saw the landing. It was an exciting moment when Neil Armstrong actually set foot on the Moon's surface—nearly 240,000 miles (386,243 kilometers) from Earth.

But the history of space travel began long before the 1960s, in the imaginations of some creative people. Two vital developments took place centuries before anyone traveled into space. In about 1200, the Chinese invented **rockets**, using gunpowder and bamboo tubes. This led some people to imagine the possibility of sending an object into the sky for long distances. Four centuries later, after the invention of the telescope, **astronomy** became a science.

Not long after the Wright Brothers made their first airplane flight in 1903, scientists speculated about going farther. In 1926, Robert H. Goddard fired the world's first liquid-fueled rocket. He helped prove that a rocket could propel itself in the vacuum of space. Goddard, a scientist and professor, is considered the father of America's space program. His ideas led to the development of rockets used by the Germans during World War II (1939–1945).

After World War II, a renowned German physicist named Dr. Wernher von Braun came to the United

States. He joined the new space program. So did other German experts. American scientists and politicians wanted to be first in space, ahead of the **Soviet Union**. In 1955, the United States declared that it would launch a **satellite** sometime in 1958. U.S. leaders knew that they could use the skills of those German experts to develop missiles for the military.

Americans were shocked on October 4, 1957. The Soviet Union launched the first artificial satellite into orbit around the Earth. It was named *Sputnik*. The launch triggered a "space race" between the two countries. Many Americans soon believed the United States had fallen behind Russia in technology.

The Soviets were winning the race to reach space. U.S. politicians called for better education, especially in science and math. The United States couldn't beat the Soviets, they insisted, unless children learned more technical subjects. Congress passed the National Defense Education Act in 1958.

The National Aeronautics and Space Administration (NASA) was created in 1958. This U.S. government agency performs aeronautics and space research. *Project Mercury* was started in 1958. It was the United States' first human spaceflight program. Project Mercury was important because it helped prove that human spaceflight was possible.

This building in Washington, DC, served as NASA headquarters from 1958 until October 1961.

President John F. Kennedy wanted the United States to reach the Moon during the 1960s. Before the Americans were ready, the Soviets made history again. On April 12, 1961, Yuri A. Gagarin entered space in the *Vostok 1* space **capsule**. Gagarin was the first human to orbit Earth and travel into space. On February 20, 1962, John Glenn became the first American to orbit Earth.

Apollo 11 launched from the Kennedy Space Center on July 16, 1969.

Another U.S. space program, *Apollo*, had a big goal: land on the Moon and return. In October 1968, *Apollo 7* went into orbit for 11 days, with three astronauts aboard. Two months later, *Apollo 8*'s astronauts were the first people to see the backside of the Moon.

Finally, the United States was ready. On July 16, 1969, a million people stood on Florida's eastern coast to watch the *Apollo 11* launch. Neil Armstrong, Michael Collins, and Edwin "Buzz" Aldrin sat scrunched inside the spaceship. Reaching lunar orbit took four days. Then a special spacecraft took Armstrong and Aldrin to the Moon's surface. Their TV camera shared the moment with the world. After setting foot on the Moon, Armstrong uttered the famous phrase: "That's one small step for a man, one giant leap for mankind." Armstrong and Aldrin set up a U.S. flag, while Collins orbited the Moon alone in the main ship. The next day, they headed back to Earth.

NASA eventually took on a new course of research, starting with the launch of the *Skylab* space station that orbited Earth between 1973 and 1979. Space became a joint mission, bringing together men and women of different cultures and ethnicities. The first partnership was the *Apollo-Soyuz* mission in 1975. For this mission, American and Soviet ships docked together in space. Thirty-five astronauts were selected for the *Space Shuttle*

21st Century Content

Valentina Tereshkova was the first woman to fly into space, in June 1963. Her ship, the *Vostok 6*, was launched by the Soviet Union. In the United States, women worked for NASA as scientists, astronomers, engineers, or mathematicians. But they were not necessarily welcomed on space flights. Eventually, that began to change. In 1983, Sally Ride became the first American woman to travel in space. She participated in a six-day flight aboard the space shuttle *Challenger*.

Space research and exploration benefits from the efforts of lots of people of different genders, races, and cultures. These people collaborate to make new discoveries. As of 2007, a total of 46 women had flown in space. Why do you think that even today, only a small number of women have traveled to space?

and *International Space Station* program in 1978. Of these, six were women and three were African Americans.

Unfortunately, advances in space travel are not without danger. Major accidents have occurred. One disaster happened in 1986. Shortly after liftoff, the shuttle *Challenger* exploded. All seven astronauts were killed, including teacher Christa McAuliffe. In 2003, the space shuttle *Columbia* developed a hole in its wing during re-entry, which caused the spacecraft to come apart. All seven crew members were killed.

Since the end of the **Cold War** in 1990, the United States and Russia have worked more closely together. In the mid-1990s, NASA sent astronauts to the Russian space station *Mir*. And in the 21st century, space travel has a promising future.

CHAPTER TWO

Advancing Technology

Through the 20th century, the development of space travel was like a set of building blocks. Each new invention built upon what came before. The evolution of space travel has depended upon the ideas of many people working together.

The invention of the telescope let people observe how planets differed from stars. In 1610, the astronomer

Space shuttle *Atlantis* is shown here attached to the *Mir Space Station*. Today, U.S. and Russian astronauts work together to make new space discoveries.

Galileo saw four of Jupiter's moons with a telescope. With the aid of telescopes, scientists learned about orbits. These are the paths objects in space follow around a planet or sun.

Complex calculations are needed when working with orbits and routes over long distances in space. The invention of computers was a huge breakthrough.

NASA's Johnson Space Center in Houston has long been the command center for NASA space flights and missions.

They could process complex data. Computers in early spaceships were enormous compared to modern ones. They were painfully slow, too. But they soon became quicker and smaller. Experts on Earth use radio signals and computers to control spaceships during flights. At times, though, the astronauts must take over.

Space lies beyond Earth's **atmosphere**, high above the planet's surface. This is higher than any airplane would be able to function in or reach. Airplanes need an atmosphere with oxygen in it to burn their fuel. Space is also colder than anywhere on Earth. It's close to absolute zero. That's approximately −459 degrees Fahrenheit (−273 degrees Celsius). Space contains no air, so fuels that require oxygen to burn cannot be used. Special fuel, in liquid or solid form, must be carried along.

Life & Career Skills

Even though so many experts work on space programs, things sometimes go wrong. Tiny parts can cause big troubles if they fail. When the *Apollo 13* team approached the Moon in 1970, an explosion threatened the mission. Commander Jim Lovell, his team on the ship, and the crew back in Houston had to think hard and come up with emergency solutions. In situations such as this one, using time efficiently is very important. It can mean the difference between life and death. They came up with a plan, and the astronauts managed to return to Earth safely. Investigators learned that a switch didn't work properly and caused the problem.

What skills do you think a person needs to succeed in situations in which there's little time and a lot of pressure?

To break free of gravity, a spaceship must travel at very high speeds. To orbit the Earth, it must reach 17,500 miles (28,164 kilometers) per hour. To burst out of orbit, toward the Moon or a planet, it has to approach 25,000 miles (40,234 km) per hour. Earth's gravity doesn't affect an object in space as strongly as when it's on the surface of the planet. That is because the pull of gravity decreases as the space shuttle travels farther from the Earth's core. While in space, objects or people in a spaceship seem to float. Intensive training is essential to help people prepare for these conditions in space.

Thousands of people have participated in NASA's space programs. Each has been an expert in some area. Working together, they created the spaceships that could handle the challenges of space travel. They also created methods to prepare people to travel in space. Today's space adventurers are usually scientists and researchers. Some are trying to reach certain destinations, such as Mars. Other 21st century astronauts want to travel to space to do experiments without the effects of gravity. Whatever the reason, people still have a strong interest in traveling to, and studying, space.

CHAPTER THREE

Space and Business

Space research and exploration serve many purposes. Obviously, space research has benefited the scientific community and led to many important discoveries. Special systems and technology used in space can be used for military purposes. But there's also a strong business interest in space.

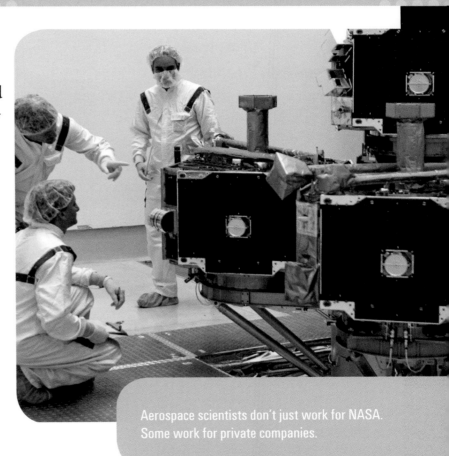

Aerospace scientists don't just work for NASA. Some work for private companies.

Businesspeople were not directly involved in trips into space, but many private companies supplied equipment and parts needed for space missions. Not long after the first satellites went into orbit, leaders in the communications industry saw possibilities. They thought that satellites could be used to greatly improve communication. Soon, engineers learned how to bounce signals off a satellite and send them back to Earth. As new technology was developed, satellites became part of daily life. Long-distance phone calls got cheaper. Radio and television stations used satellites to send their

Today, networks of satellites and satellite dishes are used for radio, television, and other forms of communication.

Many cars are now equipped with GPS systems.

programs efficiently. Satellites helped people predict the weather much more accurately.

Other creative thinkers saw that satellites could serve another purpose. They worked on developing what is now known as the Global Positioning System (GPS). A network of GPS satellites was sent into orbit by the U.S. Department of Defense. It was originally intended for military use. By the 1990s, the system was available for civilian use. These satellites circle Earth in precise orbits. They transmit signals to receivers. Anyone with a GPS

21st Century Content

How has space travel helped sell products? Even if a product wasn't invented by NASA's staff, it got publicity when used by astronauts. Tang, an orange-flavored powder that became a drink by adding water, wasn't very popular in its early years. Then astronauts started drinking it on early space missions. More people became aware of the product. Advertisers played up the connection between Tang and space. Sales increased. These days, Tang isn't as popular as it was in the 1960s and 1970s.

Companies take economic and financial risks when they introduce new products to the public. But there's a good chance people might buy something if it is associated with someone or something that people think is cool and interesting. Can you think of examples of companies that have connected a product to a famous actor or athlete?

receiver can determine his or her location, with great accuracy. GPS helps guide ships, planes, and automobiles.

Plenty of innovations have come from, or are related to, the space program. Cordless power tools were developed and used to get samples from the surface of the Moon. The technology that made these tools possible helped lead to the development of modern cordless tools. NASA scientists have developed water purification methods. This technology is important in space travel because there's a limited amount of water onboard the spaceship. NASA has also developed the technology behind scratch-resistant lenses, now used for making eyeglasses. Even the technology used for ear thermometers was originally meant for studying space.

CHAPTER FOUR

The Future of Space Travel

Astronauts continue to travel through space in the 21st century. NASA still launches spaceships from Florida. But we don't hear nearly as much about them as we did in the 1960s and 1970s. Since the *Apollo* missions, no U.S. astronaut has gone beyond a low orbit path around Earth.

Most of us have enjoyed the benefits that resulted from past space missions.

NASA employees begin the process of moving the space shuttle *Discovery* to the launch pad for its spring 2008 mission.

These include satellite-based communications. But many people aren't so sure if the benefits of doing experiments in space are worth the huge expense. No one knows if the level of excitement reached during the first "moon walk,"

U.S. astronaut Shannon Lucid exercises inside the *Mir* space station.

in 1969, will ever be matched again. Even if space travel does expand, some believe it would be wiser to use robots instead of people on future missions.

In recent years, most travel beyond Earth has involved the *International Space Station* and the space shuttles. Just after Christmas in 2007, TV showed live coverage of a shipment of food, fuel, supplies, and holiday gifts to the *International Space Station*. Shuttle trips continued into 2008, the 10th year of the Space Station's operations in orbit.

There are still plenty of youngsters who want to become astronauts or scientists. To stimulate interest in future programs, youngsters may attend U.S. Space Camp in Alabama. There kids can use equipment that re-creates astronaut training activities and the conditions in space.

Learning & Innovation Skills

There wasn't much room in the early spaceships. Astronauts in bulky space suits were stuffed into the ship's control section. They had little room to move around. Later voyages in bigger ships gave the astronauts more room to do their work. When they began to go on journeys that lasted weeks or months, they needed even more room. Even though conditions have improved, there is still less room on a spaceship than most people are used to.

Adjusting to life on a spaceship involves being open to different ways of living and working with others. That means accepting that there is less privacy. It also means finding creative and original uses for the limited space in a ship. Can you think of some other ways that life on a spaceship is different from life on Earth?

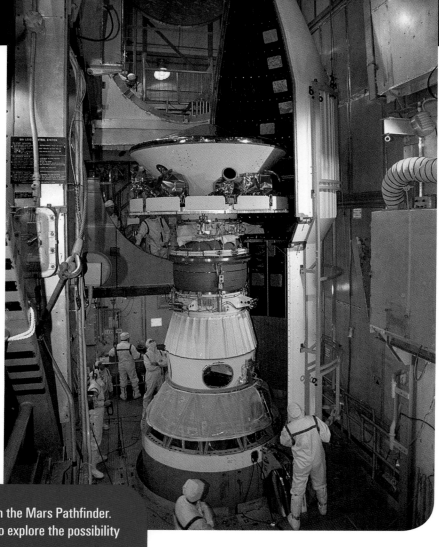

Workers do a final check on the Mars Pathfinder. NASA scientists continue to explore the possibility of a manned flight to Mars.

Some results that people hoped to achieve through space travel have not happened. No one has established colonies on the Moon. Only ships without people have traveled to other planets. But the dreams haven't ended. In September 2005, NASA announced plans to return to the Moon by 2018. There are also plans to send people

At Space Camp, kids can explore what it is like to be an astronaut.

to Mars. Much more research is needed, however, before that can become a reality. Scientists think astronauts could live on the Moon for as long as six months. They even envision using it as a base for Mars journeys. Time will tell if these ideas can actually be made to work.

In the future, you may not need to be an astronaut to visit space. Ordinary people might participate in future space excursions. In 2004, Michael Melville flew

SpaceShipOne into space. He was the first private citizen to make such a trip. It was in a privately owned rocket plane. Private groups have even been developing sun-powered spaceships. They also promise rockets that cost less than those built with government funding.

Late in 2007, BBC News reported that a South Korean space program chose an astronaut from a TV contest. A research scientist won the opportunity to travel into space.

Former astronaut Buzz Aldrin formed a company to promote space travel. His company also explores new ideas for future efforts. Businesspeople already have sold "tickets" for future space flights, but no one knows if they will ever get off the ground. But one thing is certain: space travel will continue to develop and evolve in the years to come.

CHAPTER FIVE

Famous Innovators

The development of spaceships has been largely a team effort. At NASA, many experts work together to get the job done. Still, several people stand out in the history of space exploration.

In 1992, Mae Jemison became the first African American woman to enter space.

Dr. Robert H. Goddard

Robert Goddard was among the first to envision exploration of space. As early as 1912, he used mathematics to determine if it was possible to reach high altitudes. He received patents for liquid-fueled and solid-fueled rockets. In 1926, he built and tested the first rocket using liquid fuel.

Goddard was a physics professor at Clark University in Worcester, Massachusetts.

Von Braun helped develop the rocket that launched the first U.S. satellite into space.

Dr. Wernher von Braun

In 1932, Wernher von Braun started work for the German army. After earning a doctorate in physics, he led a rocket team that developed the V-2 missile for the Nazis during World War II. He was eventually brought to the United States. For 15 years, he worked with the U.S. Army on missiles and rockets. He served as director of NASA's Marshall Space Flight Center and was chief designer of the *Saturn V* launch vehicle.

Yuri A. Gagarin

By 1959, Yuri Gagarin was selected for the first group of Soviet **cosmonauts**. On April 12, 1961, he became the first human to orbit Earth, in the *Vostok 1* ship. His flight reached about 202 miles (325 km) above the Earth's surface.

Yuri Gagarin prepares for his historic mission in 1961.

John H. Glenn Jr.

John Glenn was chosen by NASA as one of the first seven astronauts in 1959. On February 20, 1962, he became the first American to orbit Earth. He circled the globe three times. In 1998, he rejoined the space program as a crew member on the space shuttle *Discovery*. At 77 years old, that trip made him the oldest person to travel in space.

Life & Career Skills

When a spaceship is launched, everybody works together—on Earth and in space. Astronauts get the glory, but each scientist, mathematician, engineer, or technician is part of the same team. Each does very important things. Scientists, for example, improve the materials used in spaceships, the way fuel is used, and much more. It's important for everyone involved in a space mission to be able to work well with others. It's also important to be able to communicate ideas clearly. During a flight, American astronauts communicate with NASA's Johnson Space Center in Houston, Texas. Communication is important because everyone is trying to achieve a common goal. Mission goals can range from reaching the Moon to repairing a damaged piece of equipment.

Glossary

astronauts (ASS-truh-nawtss) people who are trained to travel in space

astronomy (uh-STRON-uh-mee) the study of the stars, planets, and other objects in space

atmosphere (AT-muhss-feer) the layer of gases that surrounds a planet

capsule (KAP-suhl) the portion of a spaceship in which astronauts ride

Cold War (KOHLD WOR) the state of constant tension between the United States and the Soviet Union, which lasted from 1945 to 1990; it did not result in actual warfare

cosmonauts (KAHZ-muh-nawtss) astronauts from Russia or what used to be the Soviet Union

rockets (ROK-itss) devices that are shaped like tubes and can be used to launch spacecraft

satellite (SAA-tuh-lite) an object that orbits Earth; some satellites receive or collect signals and send them back to Earth

Soviet Union (SOH-vee-et YOON-yuhn) a union of Russia and other countries in Eurasia officially known as the Union of Soviet Socialist Republics (USSR) that existed from 1922 to 1991

For More Information

BOOKS

Jefferis, David, and Mat Irvine. *Race into Space*. New York: Crabtree Publishing, 2007.

Stott, Carole. *Space Exploration*. New York: DK Publishing, 2004.

Thomson, Sarah L. *Astronauts and Other Space Heroes*. New York: Smithsonian: Collins, 2007.

WEB SITES

National Aeronautics and Space Administration (NASA)
www.nasa.gov
Find information on current and historical NASA activities

Smithsonian National Air and Space Museum
www.nasm.si.edu
Browse photos and find facts about space missions

The Space Race
www.thespacerace.com
Learn about the *Mercury*, *Gemini*, and *Apollo* space programs

Index

About the Author

James M. Flammang is a journalist and author who specializes in transportation topics. Technology is one of his primary interests. He enjoys writing about technical achievements of the past, as well as those that may come in the future. In addition to evaluating and reviewing new cars and trucks, he has written more than 20 books about the history of the automobile. His Web site, Tirekicking Today, is at www.tirekick.com. In addition to titles in the Innovation in Transportation series, he has written three previous books for young readers. Flammang lives in Elk Grove Village, Illinois.